THE ARAB-ISRAELI MILITARY BALANCE SINCE OCTOBER 1973

Dale R. Tahtinen

With a foreword by Robert P. Griffin

American Enterprise Institute for Public Policy Research
Washington, D. C.

Dale R. Tahtinen is assistant to the director of foreign and
defense policy studies of the American Enterprise Institute
for Public Policy Research.

ISBN 0-8447-3132-3

Foreign Affairs Studies No. 11

Library of Congress Catalog Card No. 74-81729

Printed in the United States of America

CONTENTS

FOREWORD

The Arab-Israeli conflict has long been the focus of international tension and periodic full-scale violence. Most recently, the October war reemphasized the volatility of this historic conflict. The continuing clashes on the Syrian and Israeli front over the past several months underline the crucial need to bring about a lasting peace. However, the issues basic to any solution of the conflict are likely to be made more complex by the increasingly sophisticated weapons that have been provided to the belligerents by their respective superpower patrons.

This study is both timely and informative because it provides one of the first comprehensive examinations of the military strength of Israel and the neighboring Arab states since October 1973. As the author points out, each Arab-Israeli war has been fought at a higher level of sophistication. If his thesis is correct, yet another large-scale outbreak of hostilities might lead to warfare that goes beyond conventional means, even to the point of direct superpower involvement.

Whether or not one fully agrees with the substance of the arguments presented in this study, a number of sobering questions are raised that might well be the subject of extensive public discussion.

Robert P. Griffin
9 May 1974

THE ARAB-ISRAELI MILITARY BALANCE
SINCE OCTOBER 1973

Introduction

World attention is once again focused on the Middle East as a source of dangerous instability. The October 1973 conflict underscored the strategic value the superpowers place on the area. The war was fought with much more sophisticated equipment than any previous Arab-Israeli conflict, and during the hostilities both the United States and the Soviet Union rushed to assist their respective "client" (a weaker state protected by a stronger one) states. Fortunately, the superpowers ultimately limited their competition to only arms resupply and the world did not suffer a nuclear holocaust. Mankind came uncomfortably close to such a fate, however, when the United States placed its armed forces on high-level alert in response to what it apparently saw as a Soviet threat to American interests in the Middle East. The latter threat may well have been what Secretary of Defense James Schlesinger described as a "peremptory Soviet note to the United States implying the possibility of direct Soviet military intervention [during the October war] with ground and air forces." [1]

The major lesson to be learned from the October war and earlier Arab-Israeli conflicts is that each new outbreak in hostilities in the Middle East occurs at a higher and more dangerous level of warfare, bringing the superpowers ever nearer to military confrontation. Thus it is particularly important that the results of the October war, along with any significant changes in the military balance and the likelihood of new hostilities in the future, should be analyzed.

---

[1] James R. Schlesinger, *Annual Defense Department Report, FY 1975* (Washington, D. C.: Government Printing Office, 1974), p. 13. There have also been reports that the U.S.S.R. placed some seven divisions on alert for possible intervention on the Egyptian front. Murray Marder, "Press Reporting '73 Soviet Alert," *Washington Post*, 2 May 1974.

Despite the absence of significant amounts of precise data regarding the exact number of different types of weapons possessed by the belligerents in the Arab-Israeli conflict, it is still possible to develop a relatively accurate picture of the present Middle East military balance as well as to show the buildup that has occurred since 1967.[2] It has been said that both sides received replacements for the equipment lost during the October hostilities and that, in many instances, the new weapons were of a more advanced variety. In the case of some weapons, the number accrued during the resupply by the two superpowers actually exceeded the number lost in the fighting.[3] Therefore, using tables reflecting the amount of weapons available to the two sides at the outbreak of hostilities, it is possible—with the use of textual additions—to establish a generally reliable estimate of the present military balance between Israel and her major Arab adversaries.

A number of important military lessons evolved from the October conflict (see the Appendix for American and Soviet perceptions). One of the most significant is that effective use of missiles has decreased the value of aircraft, tanks, and other armor, at least until such weapons are made less vulnerable to missiles.

1. Air Defense

Syria's mobile defense system on the Golan Heights stretched from ground level to some 70,000 feet, using a combination of ZSU-23 radar-controlled, quad-mounted 23-mm. cannons, SA-2, -3, -6, and -7 surface-to-air missiles (SAMs) and a top cover of MiG-21s.[4] (See Table 1 for characteristics of the major antiaircraft missile systems in use in the Middle East.) This system, and a similar but more static one on the Egyptian front, took a considerable toll of Israeli aircraft.[5] Tel Aviv's dominant air superiority, however, eventually prevailed over the Egyptian and Syrian air-defense systems because the Arab

---

[2] For detailed analysis of the arms race from 1967 to the October war, see Dale R. Tahtinen, *The Arab-Israeli Military Balance Today* (Washington, D. C.: American Enterprise Institute, October 1973).

[3] See testimony by Admiral Thomas H. Moorer, chairman, Joint Chiefs of Staff, and William P. Clements, Jr., deputy secretary of defense, *Emergency Security Assistance Act of 1973*, Hearings before the Committee on Foreign Affairs, U.S. House of Representatives, 93rd Congress, 1st session, 30 November and 3 December 1973.

[4] Robert Hotz, "The lessons of October," *Aviation Week and Space Technology*, 3 December 1973, p. 13.

[5] Ibid.

Table 1

MAJOR SURFACE-TO-AIR MISSILES [a]

Type	Characteristics	Effective Ceiling (feet)
SA-2	The SA-2 is a two-stage missile with automatic radio command. Target aircraft are tracked by radar which feeds signals to a computer, from which radio signals to the missile are generated. Those captured by the Israelis in 1967 had warheads detonated by contact or proximity fuses. American pilots in Vietnam have reported that the SA-2s there lack the maneuverability needed to intercept high-speed aircraft performing evasive tight turns.	60,000
SA-3	The SA-3 is a two-stage, compact, mobile land-based missile used for short-range defense against aircraft to very low altitudes. It is similar to the American-made Hawk used by Israel.	40,000
SA-6	This missile is considerably larger than the American-built Hawk but is assumed to have the same basic low-altitude defense role. Each unit consists of a tracked vehicle with three solid propellant missiles.	Unknown
Hawk	This is an American-made guided weapon with a solid-propellant motor and a continuous-wave, semi-active radar-homing system. It is said to be effective against aircraft flying at normal combat altitudes down to tree-top level.	Over 38,000

[a] Not included are shoulder-fired guided missiles used for defense against low-flying aircraft.

Source: *Jane's All The World's Aircraft, 1972-1973* and *1971-1972*.

MiGs were simply no match for the more advanced and better piloted Israeli planes and because the Israelis used fairly effective electronic countermeasure (ECM) gear. Recognizing the need for such equipment, the United States supplied the Israelis ECM equipment more advanced than that carried by their planes prior to the eruption of hostilities (see Table 2). In addition, American ECM experts were reportedly sent to Israel during the war.[6] The new ECM gear, how-

---

[6] "U.S. Spurs Countermeasures to Israel," *Aviation Week and Space Technology*, 22 October 1973, p. 20; Barry Miller, "U.S. Equips Israel with 'Smart' Guided Weapons," *Aviation Week and Space Technology*, 5 November 1973, p. 18; and David Loehwing, "The Deadly Black Boxes," *Barron's*, 4 February 1974, p. 5.

Table 2

CHARACTERISTICS OF SOME MAJOR ECM SYSTEMS IN THE MIDDLE EAST

Type	Characteristics
ALQ-71	The ALQ-71 contains subsystems for noise jamming in the L-, S-, and C-bands of the radar spectrum. Separate units incorporate pairs of jammers for the three separate radar bands. Blade antennae on the underside of the equipment pod radiate noise signals. ALQ-71 provides both horizontally and vertically polarized signals. The system is used on F-4 and other aircraft and is designed to give protection against air surveillance radars and surface-to-air missiles. ALQ-71 has reportedly been adapted to meet higher-frequency threats such as that posed by the SA-3's I-band Low Blow radar.
ALQ-119	The system was reportedly developed relatively recently to meet the Soviet threat to NATO and is a more sophisticated version of the ALQ-71. The pods which are fitted to the F-4 contain modulated noise jammers and are said to have a sufficient broadband capability to be effective against the SA-6.
ALQ-87	The system is a standard tactical jammer that was used by F-4s in their raids over North Vietnam in the last year of direct American military involvement in Southeast Asia.
ALE-29	The ALE-29 is comprised of a thirty-two cartridge dispenser of chaff to shield attacking aircraft from radar-directed weapons. ALE-29 is fitted to A-4s. The Israelis have also fired flares from ALE-29 dispensers to decoy the heat-seeking Soviet-made SA-7s.
ALE-38	This is a bulk chaff dispenser which is capable of dropping 300 pounds of metalized glass or aluminum chaff to protect attacking aircraft. The pod can be attached to an F-4 wing pylon, as was done for American raids over Hanoi.
QRC-335-4	This system was deployed by the USAF in 1969 and reflects a modification of the digital automatic ECM system on the F-4/RF-4 reconnaissance aircraft (of which Israel has six). This gives a capability for X-band jamming.

Source: *Jane's Weapon Systems, 1972-1973;* "U.S. Spurs Countermeasures to Israel," *Aviation Week and Space Technology,* 22 October 1973, p. 20; "U.S. Girds for Survival in Electronic Warfare," *Aviation Week and Space Technology,* 21 February 1972, p. 73; and "Strong ECM Market Found Abroad," *Aviation Week and Space Technology,* 19 October 1970, p. 63.

ever, was not completely effective against the SA-6 and SA-7. The latter is a shoulder-fired SAM that homes in on aircraft exhausts. It is particularly effective when an attacking plane is at an altitude where ECMs are not usually operating.[7] No ECM device has been developed to effectively jam the operation of such a weapon.

[7] "SA-7 Avoids Homing on Flares," *Aviation Week and Space Technology,* 5 November 1973, p. 17.

The success of the Syrian and Egyptian air defenses against what may be some of the best American ECM hardware has spurred a vigorous research and development effort in the United States to develop more effective countermeasures.[8] But even with better ECMs, the number of planes lost will probably continue to be high enough to cause a client state such as Israel to place heavy reliance upon its superpower patron for direct grant assistance to cover the cost of new aircraft.

The ECM situation is particularly instructive in several ways. First, it indicates that the sophistication of the conflict has reached such a level that Israel must rely more heavily than ever before on the best equipment available in the inventory of the United States.[9] This in turn means the Arabs will probably go to the Soviet Union for weapons that will be effective against Israeli acquisitions. The second lesson is that to pursue such weapons is tremendously expensive, and while the Arab states can count on oil revenues to pay for much of their equipment the Israelis cannot. Therefore, the longer the Middle East conflict lasts the more expensive it will become for the United States as it is importuned to supply greater amounts of advanced weaponry to Israel.

Another interesting point is that one can hardly accuse the Soviet Union of escalating the Arab-Israeli arms race by providing an effective air-defense system that challenges some of the best American ECMs. On the contrary, the United States had some time ago furnished Israel with a highly effective air-defense system which is said to be at least equivalent to, if not better than, the Soviet-built interlaced SAM system.[10]

Alternative Air Offenses. Given the greater cost in terms of potential aircraft losses, the use of other delivery systems might become more attractive to Tel Aviv. For instance, the use of pilotless drones to deliver bombs against missile sites, other military installations, and even civilian populations becomes a more alluring alternative as long as there is a very high probability of losing multimillion-dollar air-

---

[8] For instance, see "Pentagon Spurs SA-6 Countermeasure," *Aviation Week and Space Technology*, 5 November 1973, p. 17.

[9] Several American ECM companies even conduct domestic operations in Israel (Barry Miller, "Strong ECM Market Found Abroad," *Aviation Week and Space Technology*, 19 October 1970, p. 67).

[10] "Neither Side Armed with a Single Knock-out Weapon," *Manchester Guardian*, 17 October 1973. To improve its air defense even more, Israel has reportedly renewed attempts to procure the American E-3A airborne warning and control aircraft (*Aviation Week and Space Technology*, 1 April 1974, p. 11).

craft in any strike against opposition targets. For instance, against an even better air-defense system protecting Damascus than existed in October 1973, future Israeli air strikes may well be accomplished by using drones rather than aircraft. Another possibility is to use pilotless craft against SAM sites to sanitize a corridor for attacking aircraft.[11]

A third, and considerably more expensive, alternative is to use surface-to-surface missiles to deliver high-explosive conventional ordnance or nuclear bombs. On the Arab side, the surface-to-surface Scud missile might be a particularly attractive weapon because Syrian and Egyptian pilots, with their less sophisticated planes, would have only a slim chance of penetrating Israel's highly effective American-supplied Hawk air-defense system. Furthermore, a number of surface-to-surface missiles could rain considerable destruction upon Israel's industry, population, and storage facilities concentrated in the Haifa-Jaffa-Tel Aviv triangle, even if only some of the weapons reached their targets with high-explosive conventional warheads.

In terms of comparative missile numbers, the Israelis appear to hold a significant advantage. Tel Aviv reportedly has some sixty domestically produced 300-mile range Jericho surface-to-surface missiles.[12] Egypt is said to have about twenty Soviet-built Scud missiles—probably acquired in October—with approximately a 180-mile range, plus an unknown number of Frog-7 and the older Frog-3 surface-to-surface missiles with ranges of some twenty-five and thirty-five miles, respectively.[13] Syria is also reported to have Scud and Frog-7 missiles.[14] The exact number of these weapons is not known, but it would be surprising if Damascus was given a greater number of Scuds than Cairo. Egypt has also attempted to produce surface-to-surface missiles but without any known success.

---

[11] The Israelis are reported to have a number of drones which have been modified to carry two 500-pound bombs, to act as a radar jammer or to simulate an attacking plane to draw SAM fire before manned aircraft arrive. William Beecher, "Watch on the Suez: Israel Weighs the Options," Army, December 1971, p. 3.

[12] Tahtinen, Arab-Israeli Balance, p. 33. Also, see Dana Adams Schmidt, "Mideast Nuclear Stockpile," Christian Science Monitor, 23 November 1973.

[13] Ibid. Estimates vary from 160 to 200 miles on the range of the Scud. Also, see International Institute for Strategic Studies, The Military Balance, 1973-1974 (London, 1973), p. 31, and Jane's Weapon Systems, 1972-1973 (New York: McGraw-Hill Book Company, 1972), pp. 34-35.

[14] David Hirst, "The Hawks Could Still Bring Back War," Manchester Guardian, 26 January 1974. Also, see "Attacks on Civilian Prompted Bombing," London Times, 10 October 1973.

Aircraft. Although better air defenses have made the use of aircraft considerably more expensive, air superiority will still be very important in any future Middle East conflict (see Table 3). Despite heavy aircraft losses during the October war (which were quickly replaced), Tel Aviv was able to begin to turn the battle tide once it had made progress in breaking the air-defense belt on both the Syrian and Egyptian fronts.[15]

Both sides are said to have received replacements for their air losses during the war, and in some cases, as with ECMs, the resupply brought more sophisticated equipment into the area. This was also apparently the case in terms of the number of aircraft delivered. For instance, total Israeli plane losses have been placed at about 110 aircraft, including about thirty-five F-4 Phantoms,[16] but Tel Aviv is said to have received forty of the aircraft during the resupply operation.[17] Other sources have reported that late in the war the United States was already "planning to fly in some forty-eight Phantoms."[18] It is also possible that a similar situation has occurred with the A-4 Skyhawk, of which some fifty-five were lost,[19] but in the latter part of the war the United States Marines had reportedly been told to prepare eighty of their A-4s for delivery to Israel.[20] Other Israeli losses will probably be replaced internally: for the dozen Mirage III casualties,[21] a similar aircraft, the Israeli-produced Barak fighter, which had initial combat experience in October, could be substituted. Israel's air force reportedly had already acquired some twenty-five Baraks before the outbreak of hostilities in October.[22] It has been said that Tel Aviv's air inventory will soon be 80 percent higher than before the October conflict.[23]

---

[15] Herbert J. Coleman, "Israeli Air Force Decisive in War," *Aviation Week and Space Technology*, 3 December 1973, p. 18. Also, see Hotz, "Lessons of October," p. 13.

[16] Coleman, "Air Force Decisive in War," p. 18.

[17] Cecil Brownlow, "Soviet Poise Three-Front Global Drive," *Aviation Week and Space Technology*, 5 November 1973, p. 14.

[18] "700 Tons a Day to Each Side," *Economist*, 20 October 1973, p. 35.

[19] Coleman, "Air Force Decisive in War," p. 18.

[20] Fred Emery, "North Korean Pilots in Egypt MiGs Open Fire on Israelis," *London Times*, 19 October 1973.

[21] Coleman, "Air Force Decisive in War," p. 18.

[22] "Barak in Combat," *Aviation Week and Space Technology*, 15 October 1973, p. 12. Also, see Tahtinen, *Arab-Israeli Balance*, pp. 9-10.

[23] Joseph Fried, "If It's War, Israel Holds Edge," *New York Daily News*, 10 March 1974. Early last November Israel was reportedly already planning to double the size of its tank and air forces. See Charles W. Corddry, "Israel Said to Want to Double Size of Tank and Air Forces," *Baltimore Sun*, 8 November 1973.

Table 3

COMBAT AIRCRAFT INVENTORIES IN THE MIDDLE EAST PRIOR TO OCTOBER WAR

Country/Aircraft Type	1967-68a	1968-69	1969-70	1970-71	1971-72	1972-73	1973b
Egypt							
MiG-21 interceptor	100	110	100	150	200	220	210
MiG-19 all-weather fighter	45	80	—	—	—	—	—
Su-7 fighter-bomber	—	40	90	105	110	120	80
MiG-15 fighter	{ 60	120	120	165 }	—	—	—
MiG-17 fighter-bomber					200	200	100
Il-28 light bomber	20	40	30	28	25	10	5
Tu-16 medium bomber	—	10	12	15	18	18	25
MiG, Yak, L-29 Trainers (can be armed)	—	—	—	—	—	—	200
Total	225	400	352	463	553	568	620
Syria							
MiG-21 interceptor	—	60	55	90	100	140	200
Su-7 fighter-bomber	—	20	20	40	30	30	30
MiG-17 day fighter/ground attack	—	—	—	—	—	80	80
MiG-15 fighter	25	70	70	80	80	80	—
Il-28 light bomber	—	—	—	—	—	—	—c
Total	25	150	145	210	210	250	310d
Jordan							
Hunter ground attack	—	12	11	20	18	35	32
F-104A fighter-bomber	—	—	—	18	15	15	20
F-86	—	4	—	—	—	—	—
Total	—	16	11	38	33	50	52e

Iraq

MiG-21 interceptor	50	60	60	85	80	90
Su-7 fighter-bomber	—	20	50	48	48	60
MiG-19 fighter	{ 34	{ 45	{ 45	—	—	30
MiG-17 fighter-bomber				15	20	—
Tu-16 medium bomber	6	8	8	9	9	8
Il-28 light bomber	10	10	10	12	—	—
Hunter ground attack	50	50	36	35	32	36
T-52 light strike	20	20	20	16	—	—
Total	170	213	229	220	189	224[f]

Libya

Mirage V and 111B/C/E ground attack and interceptor	—	—	—	—	72	110[g]
F-5A interceptor	—	—	7	7	10	9
Total	—	—	7	7	82	119

Algeria

MiG-21 interceptor	—	{ 140	{ 140	30	30	35
MiG-15, -17 fighter-bomber	—			60	95	95
Su-7 fighter-bomber	—	—	—	—	—	20
Il-28 light jet bomber	—	30	30	24	30	30
Magister armed trainer	—	—	—	28	26	26
Total	—	170	170	142	181	206

Saudi Arabia

BAC-167 ground attack	—	—	24	20	20	—
Lightning fighter	4	28	35	20	35	—
Hunter ground attack	4	4	—	—	—	—
F-86 fighter	12	11	16	15	15	—
Total	20	43	75	55	70[h]	—

Table 3 *(continued)*

Country/Aircraft Type	1967-68[a]	1968-69	1969-70	1970-71	1971-72	1972-73	1973[b]
Israel							
F-4 fighter-bomber/interceptor	—	—	—	36	75	120	127
A-4 fighter-bomber	—	48	48	67	72	125	162
Mirage III fighter-bomber/interceptor	65	65	65	60	60	50	35
Barak fighter	—	—	—	—	—	—	25 [i]
Vautour light bomber	15	15	15	12	10	10	12
Mystere IVA fighter-bomber	25	35	35	30	27	27	23
Oragan fighter-bomber	50	45	35	30	30	30	30
Super Mystere interceptor	25	15	12	10	9	9	18
Magister trainer with limited ground attack capability	50	65	65	85	85	85	85
Total	230	288	275	330	368	456	517

[a] All data in this table and those following are generally from 30 June to 30 June.
[b] Unless otherwise noted the figures for 1973 in this and succeeding tables represent approximate strengths at the time of the outbreak of hostilities in October.
[c] The exact number is not known but is about fifteen to twenty (see *Military Balance 1973-74*, p. 36).
[d] Syria may be flying some Su-20s since they reportedly were seen on that front during the October war.
[e] Thirty-six F-5E fighters are on order.
[f] This does not include Tu-22s flown to Iraq by Soviet pilots. There is no evidence to confirm these aircraft are being turned over to Baghdad.
[g] France reportedly delivered the last of the 110 Mirages in March 1974.
[h] Saudi Arabia may have already received a few of the 140 F-5Es on order.
[i] "Barak in Combat," *Aviation Week and Space Technology*, 15 October 1973, p. 12.

Source: International Institute for Strategic Studies, *The Military Balance 1967-1968* (London, 1967), and succeeding issues through 1973-1974.

The only available information regarding the Soviet resupply to Arab air forces is that the U.S.S.R. has sent in enough equipment to replace the high losses of the October hostilities.[24] Some 425 aircraft were reportedly lost by the Arab forces,[25] and although a type breakdown of the planes lost is not available, there is no reliable evidence that the Soviets have supplied their client states with any significant number of newer type aircraft beyond the Su-7 and various versions of the MiG-21.

Qualitative Comparisons. Israel has the same general overall advantage in the air as before the war. Assuming that Israel, Egypt, Syria, and Jordan could use every combat aircraft in their inventories (taking into account the twenty-five Baraks), Tel Aviv could deliver a maximum of some 2,100 tons of ordnance in a single strike, while the three Arab states could only muster a first-strike ordnance delivery capacity of some 1,000 tons—less than 40 percent of Israel's. The advantage could not be eliminated even if all the combat aircraft of Algeria, Iraq, Libya, and Saudi Arabia were included.

Of course, another factor of considerable importance in any such comparison is the number of sorties a day per plane that each side can fly during hostilities. Once again the Israelis hold an advantage. Their turnaround time (the time it takes to refuel and reload a plane) does not appear to have changed significantly from the 1967 war when they were getting an average of eight sorties a day per plane, and the Arabs do not seem to have exceeded the optimistic 1967 Egyptian expectations of four per day.[26] The skill of Israel's ground crews, which permits a greater number of sorties to be flown per day, gives Tel Aviv an even greater edge in ordnance delivery capability than the absolute figures above indicate.

An additional qualitative factor is the comparatively greater range of Israel's combat aircraft (see Table 4). Other than the Libyan Mirage Vs, the Arab forces do not have a highly developed supersonic combat plane which can deliver a sizable amount of ordnance on targets in Israel.[27] The October war demonstrated the inability

---

24 Testimonies of Moorer and Clements, *Emergency Security Assistance Act.*

25 Coleman, "Air Force Decisive in War," p. 18.

26 Geoffrey Kemp, *Arms and Security: The Egypt-Israel Case,* Adelphi Paper No. 52 (London: Institute for Strategic Studies, October 1968).

27 This lack of equally sophisticated aircraft by the Arabs was probably at least partly responsible for what Egyptian President Anwar Sadat referred to as the targeting of surface-to-surface missiles against three main Israeli cities during the October conflict. See his interview with Arnaud de Borchgrave, "Sadat's Vision of the Future," *Newsweek,* 25 March 1974, p. 45.

Table 4

TECHNICAL CHARACTERISTICS OF MAJOR ADVANCED AIRCRAFT IN THE MIDDLE EAST

Aircraft Type	Ordnance Capability[a] (tons)	Approximate Combat Radius (miles)	Avionics, Weaponry and Operational Role
MiG-25[b]	Unknown	700	Little is known about the avionics, but the aircraft was probably designed to intercept fast strike aircraft, possibly with "snap-down" missiles to deal with low-flying raiders. It presumably carries air-to-air guided weapons.
MiG-21	.6	350	The MiG-21 is fitted with search-and-track plus warning radar and Atoll air-to-air missiles with a probable infrared guidance system similar to the American-made Sidewinder 1A.
Su-20[b]	Unknown	Unknown	The Su-20 has been referred to as a variable-geometry fighter version of the Su-11.[c] Little detailed information is available regarding this relatively new plane. The Su-11 was possibly developed to meet the Soviet requirement for a faster interceptor to replace the Su-9. Normally it carries one radar homing and one infrared homing Anab air-to-air missile. There are provisions for additional weapons or fuel.
Su-7	2.2	200-300	Subsequent to 1961, the Su-7 became the standard tactical fighter-bomber of the Soviet air force. Little information is available concerning the avionics of the Su-7.
Mirage V	4.4	400-805	The Mirage V can carry one Matra R-530 all-weather air-to-air missile with radar or infrared homing heads, an air-to-surface missile, and two Sidewinder air-to-air missiles. Avionics include air-to-air interception radar with an additional mode for control from the ground and a sighting system giving air-to-air capabilities for cannons and missiles and an air-to-ground capability for dive bombing.
F-4E	8	900-1,000	The F-4E uses highly sophisticated electronic countermeasures equipment, computers, and radar in its role as a long-range all-weather attack fighter. It is considered to be the best operational American missile-armed aircraft.
A-4E	5	400-800[d]	The A-4E fighter-bomber is equipped with an angle-of-attack indicator, terrain-clearance radar, and a variety of optional sophisticated weapons such as air-to-air and air-to-surface rockets (Sidewinders; infrared Bullpup, air-to-surface missiles and torpedoes).

Mirage IIIC	1	560-745[e]	The characteristics of the Mirage IIIC are the same as for the Mirage V, except that the planes supplied to Israel are said to have a different electronic configuration. Israel has developed an infrared homing air-to-air missile with a "see-and-shoot" capability and has fitted it to its Mirage fighters.[e]
F-14[b]	Unknown	Unknown	The F-14 is a variable-geometry fighter designed with emphasis on developing a comparatively small, lightweight high-performance aircraft that would represent a significant advance over the F-4 Phantom and the latest Soviet combat plane. The F-14 can carry armaments such as the Sparrow and Phoenix air-to-air missiles and Condor air-to-surface stand-off missiles. The F-14 Phoenix missile system is said to have been successfully tested not only against air-to-surface and surface-to-surface missiles and extreme high-altitude/high-speed interceptors, but also against four targets in a simultaneous four-missile launch. An extensive variety of sophisticated electronic systems is also carried by the F-14.
F-15[b]	Unknown	Unknown	The F-15 was designed for an air superiority role but also possesses an air-to-surface attack capability and is capable of deploying a variety of air-to-air weapons in short and medium ranges. The aircraft is also equipped with a variety of highly advanced electronic gear.

[a] The figures given based on normal weapons loads.

[b] Although the MiG-25 and Su-20 are not yet known to be in the possession of any Arab state, and the F-14 and F-15 are similarly not yet in the Israeli inventory, they could soon be provided to those states.

[c] "Soviet Aid Sparks Arab Gains," *Aviation Week and Space Technology*, 15 October 1973, p. 13.

[d] With no weapons the radius is about 1,000 miles, according to *Jane's All the World's Aircraft, 1972-1973*.

[e] "Shafrir Geared to See-and-Shoot Role," *Aviation Week and Space Technology*, 28 May 1973, p. 134.

Source: Unless otherwise noted, information was derived from *Jane's All the World's Aircraft, 1968-1969, 1972-1973, 1973-1974,* and *Jane's Weapon Systems, 1972-1973.*

of Arab aircraft to penetrate the Israeli air-defense system. It is also significant that the shorter range of Arab planes requires bases closer to Israel, which means that Tel Aviv's air force would have to concern itself with attacking fewer airfields during any future hostilities. Even the Mirage Vs would have to operate from Egyptian, Syrian, or Jordanian bases. If the Arab air forces are to match or exceed the equipment capability of Israel they would have to obtain large numbers of MiG-25 Foxbat aircraft, but the Soviets have thus far been reluctant to provide these planes to their client states.

In terms of combat radii, Tel Aviv appears to have an additional advantage: at least two airborne tankers to carry out in-flight refueling. Tel Aviv can now strike at Arab targets far beyond the normal combat radius of its already superior American-supplied planes. Comparatively, none of the major Arab powers is known to have such a refueling capability.

Such factors are critical in any analysis of relative air power and highlight the fact that one cannot compare only quantities of aircraft. To do so, one risks presenting a distorted picture. For example, when comparing numbers of aircraft only, Israel appears to be at a sizable disadvantage, but when the capabilities of the planes are compared, the Israeli air force is vastly superior. Furthermore, when combined with the human factor—effective, experienced personnel both on the ground and in the air—the Israeli advantage bulges even more.

A perfect example of the latter factor is the number of qualified pilots available. Here again, the Arabs remain at both a qualitative and quantitative disadvantage. Since October, this weakness may have tilted even further in Tel Aviv's favor because, with the reported loss of over 370 Arab aircraft in air-to-air combat,[28] it is reasonable to assume that a large number of more experienced Arab pilots were lost. Thus Israel probably increased its relative prewar edge of 800 to 900 pilots versus a total of 600 to 700 qualified pilots for Egypt, Syria, Jordan and Iraq.[29] Even the use of some thirty North Korean pilots[30] during the war did not make a significant difference. Indeed, these Arab acquisitions may have been more than offset by Israel's reported attempt to recruit experienced American pilots.[31]

---

[28] Coleman, "Air Force Decisive in War," p. 18.

[29] Martin J. Miller, Jr., "The Israeli Air Force," *Ordnance*, September-October 1972, p. 128.

[30] "Koreans over Sinai," *Aviation Week and Space Technology*, 22 October 1973, p. 25. Also, see Emery, "North Korean Pilots."

[31] Joseph Volz, "Israel Recruits Here," *Evening Star and Daily News*, 19 October 1973.

14

Tel Aviv also holds another very important advantage vis-à-vis its Arab adversaries. The Israelis, with their well-developed technological base, are able to alter imported aircraft and associated weapons, tailoring them to the unique needs of their armed forces. This capability also enables Israel to produce some of its own aircraft. Such efforts are typified by Tel Aviv's recent configuration of the domestically built Arava transport aircraft as a gunship and paratroop carrier and the production of the Barak fighter which is powered by a General Electric engine manufactured under license in Israel.[32] Israel has also developed its own air-to-air missile, Shafrir,[33] and, as previously mentioned, made significant alterations on the American-made Ryan Firebee remote-controlled reconnaissance drone. (It should be noted that neither the Arava nor the drones were included in the above computation of ordnance delivery capability.)

Other Air Weapons. As was mentioned previously, each Arab-Israeli war seems to be fought at a much higher level of sophistication, and, if there is another outbreak in hostilities, it promises to follow this pattern. Indeed, in addition to the surface-to-surface missiles already in the area, the array of other air weapons available or being requested is awesome.

For instance, during the war and the resupply effort which continued after the cease-fire, the United States sent a number of airborne versions of the tube-launched, optically tracked, wire-guided (TOW) antitank weapons to Israel.[34] Tel Aviv reportedly enjoyed a 100 percent hit record with this sophisticated weapon.[35]

Washington also provided Tel Aviv with stand-off weapons such as Hobo, Rockeye, Maverick, and Walleye 1.[36] The last item is an unpowered bomb "with wing-fins and TV-guidance system to provide a lengthened trajectory to obtain a degree of stand-off

---

[32] The Arava was in action in the recent conflict primarily as an evacuation aircraft and to ferry officers to the front. The Barak also made its debut by flying top cover in an air superiority role. See Nicolas Ashford, "Do-It-Yourself Arms Prove Their Worth to Israel," *London Times*, 26 October 1973, and Coleman, "Air Force Decisive in War," p. 18.

[33] The Shafrir was also operational in the October war. It is said to cost only about one-third the price of the French Matra air-to-air missile (Ashford, "Arms Prove Their Worth").

[34] Miller, "U.S. Equips Israel." Some 2,000 TOWs were reportedly shipped to Israel ("U.S. Soviets Boost Mideast Airlift," *Aviation Week and Space Technology*, p. 18).

[35] Ibid.

[36] Ibid., and Hotz, "Lessons of October," p. 13.

capability."[37] The Hobo (homing bomb system), a conventional bomb with a guidance and control system for greater accuracy, is sometimes referred to as a "smart bomb."[38] The Maverick is a television-guided tactical missile with a high-explosive warhead, and is designed for use against targets such as armored vehicles, concrete fortifications, gun positions, parked aircraft, and revetments.[39] Little information is available concerning the Rockeye, but it and the Maverick and Hobo are said to have achieved a remarkable 95 percent hit rate, completely destroying the tanks they hit.[40] Undoubtedly the Israeli acquisition of an electro-optical target identification system (TISEO) from the United States was also of significant assistance, since it not only identifies friend from foe at 2.6 miles from the viewer, but also assists crews in identifying ground targets at much greater ranges than is visually possible.[41]

Encouraged by the amazing success rate of these weapons, the Israelis would like to further increase the margin of sophistication between themselves and the Arabs and accordingly have reportedly requested laser-guided bombs from the United States.[42] Theoretically, these weapons should be even more accurate than those mentioned above.[43]

If such weapons find their way into the Middle East, it will merely increase the costliness of war both in terms of human suffering and material loss. For instance, the October hostilities witnessed the use of phosphorous and antipersonnel bombs. These bombs were reportedly used by Israel during the air attacks on Damascus and other Syrian targets, resulting in considerable destruction and some 700 civilian casualties.[44] The attacks were said to be in reaction to the firing of some Frog missiles into Israel from Syria.[45]

---

[37] *Jane's Weapon Systems, 1972-1973*, p. 122.

[38] Ibid., p. 123.

[39] Ibid., p. 124.

[40] Miller, "U.S. Equips Israel," p. 18.

[41] Ibid. Like some of the stand-off weapons the TISEO was not previously shipped abroad or, at least, only selectively to NATO countries.

[42] Marilyn Berger, "Dayan Presents Israeli Position on Suez Pullback," *Washington Post*, 5 January 1974.

[43] *Jane's Weapon Systems, 1972-1973*, pp. 121-122.

[44] Hirst, "Hawks Could Bring War." Such destruction was described by John P. Richardson, president, American Near East Refugee Aid, in a Cosmos Club speech in Washington, D. C., on 22 January 1974. Richardson had only recently returned from the Middle East after conducting an inspection tour to assess refugee needs. Also, see his article, "Arab Civilians and the October War," *Journal of Palestine Studies*, Winter 1974, pp. 122-129.

[45] "Attacks on Civilians Prompted Bombings," *London Times*, 10 October 1973.

To gain effective air superiority much faster and with fewer plane losses, the Israelis reportedly have also requested the United States to provide them with the recently developed Condor air-to-surface stand-off missile.[46] This missile-defense suppressor weapon with a high-explosive warhead of unknown size can be effectively fired against SAM sites while the launching aircraft is well out of the missile-defense belt.[47] Such a weapon would give Israel a tremendous advantage and would undoubtedly spur the Soviets to provide more air-to-surface weapons to their Arab clients. In the October war the Arabs reportedly expended some twenty-five Soviet-made Kelt air-to-surface stand-off missiles against Israeli targets. Twenty of the Kelts were destroyed by Israeli fighters and flak, but two radar sites and a supply depot were said to have been hit in the Sinai.[48]

Another new piece of air weaponry that may find its way into the Middle East conflict is the American Lance surface-to-surface missile system, which can be used to carry either nuclear or high-explosive conventional warheads, although it is an extremely expensive system to use in a nonnuclear capacity. Israeli Defense Minister Moshe Dayan requested the Lance system during his first visit to Washington following the cease-fire,[49] but was not reported to have it as a high priority item on his list during his second visit. If the Lance were sent to Israel, that country would be one of the first to receive the system.

In sum, there appears to be renewed emphasis on increasing the size and sophistication of military arsenals in the Middle East.[50] Having tasted some success in regaining territories seized by Israel in 1967, the Arabs were quickly rearmed by the Soviet Union, while the United States rushed to reequip Israel's air force with even more advanced and effective equipment. Thus, in terms of air power, the vicious circle of a classic arms race continues, with Israel holding a significant lead, with the added danger of a possibility of an even

---

[46] Berger, "Dayan Presents Israeli Position," and Barry Miller, "Mideast War Spurs Renewed Interest in Stand-Off Weapons," *Aviation Week and Space Technology*, 10 December 1973, p. 15. Recent reports indicate that Israel may soon receive $700 million in credits from the United States to purchase additional American military equipment. See John Finney, "700-Million More Aid to Israel Likely," *New York Times*, 1 April 1974.

[47] *Jane's Weapon Systems, 1972-1973*, pp. 121-122.

[48] Coleman, "Air Force Decisive in War," p. 21.

[49] "Buyers and Sellers," *Aviation Week and Space Technology*, 10 December 1973.

[50] The Israelis have requested even greater numbers of F-4 Phantom and A-4 Skyhawk aircraft.

more costly future conflict in which sizable military and civilian losses must be anticipated particularly if surface-to-surface missiles are used.

2. Mobile Ground Forces

If it is to be effective, any modern military force must be able to seize and maintain the initiative in ground combat. The ability to move troops, equipment and supplies on the ground through, over, and beyond enemy lines is still necessary to achieve military success. In the Middle East, Israel's highly mobile ground forces, enjoying the protection and assistance of its air force, have achieved considerable military success, particularly in the 1967 preemptive war. Since that time both sides have placed considerable emphasis upon increasing their helicopter inventories (see Tables 5 and 6).

Table 5

HELICOPTER INVENTORIES IN THE MIDDLE EAST PRIOR TO THE OCTOBER WAR

Country/Aircraft Type	1967-68	1973
Egypt		
Mi-4 and Mi-6	30	—
Mi-1, 4, 6 and 8	—	190
Syria		
Mi-1	7	? a
Mi-4	3	? a
Mi-8	—	? a
Total	10	50
Jordan		
Alouette III	4	6
Whirlwind	4	3
Total	8	9
Iraq		
Mi-1	—	—
Mi-4	9	35
Mi-8	—	29
Alouette III	—	5
Wessex	11	—
Total	20	69

Libya[b]		
AB-206	—	2
OH-13	—	3
Alouette III	—	10
Super Frelon	—	9
Total	—	24
Algeria		
Mi-1	—	4
Mi-4	50[c]	42
Hughes 269A	—	6
SA-330	—	5
Total	50	57
Saudi Arabia		
Alouette III	2	1
AB-204	—	1
AB-205	—	8
AB-206	—	20
Total	2	30
Israel		
CH-53G	—	12
UH-1D Iroquois	—	25
AB-205	—	20
Super Frelon		12
Alouette II	40	—
S-58		—
Total	40	69

a Number is unknown.
b In the summer of 1970 Libya had some helicopters, including three Alouette IIs. *(Military Balance 1969-1970.)*
c 1969-1970 was earliest information available.
Source: *Military Balance 1967-1968, 1969-1970,* and *1973-1974.*

The importance of air superiority to the achievement of such mobility is reflected by losses sustained by the belligerents in the October conflict. Israel, which held control of the skies once the SAM belts were broken, reportedly lost six helicopters, while the Arab forces lost forty.[51] Thus, despite Arab superiority in

---

[51] Coleman, "Air Force Decisive in War," p. 18.

Table 6

CHARACTERISTICS OF MAJOR HELICOPTERS IN THE MIDDLE EAST

Type	Characteristics
UH-1D Iroquois	The Iroquois can carry a pilot and twelve troops and has a maximum takeoff and landing weight of 9,500 lbs.
AB-205A	The AB-205A is a multi-purpose helicopter similar to the UH-1D. The AB-205A can carry up to fourteen passengers plus pilot and has a maximum takeoff weight of 10,500 lbs.
AB-206A	The AB-206A carries four passengers in addition to the pilot and has a cruising speed of 130 mph with a weight of some 3,000 lbs.
AB-212	The standard accommodation of the AB-212 is fourteen passengers and pilot. The aircraft can carry up to 11,200 lbs., and its cruising speed is 127 mph.
CH-53	The CH-53 accommodates two pilots plus thirty-eight troops and has a maximum takeoff weight of about 42,000 lbs.
Mi-8	The Mi-8 carries two pilots and twenty-eight to thirty-two passengers. This transport helicopter has a cruising speed of 112 to 140 mph.
Mi-6	The Mi-6 is a transport helicopter which carries a crew of five and up to sixty-five passengers. Maximum cruising speed is 155 mph.
Super Frelon	The Super Frelon carries a crew of two plus twenty-seven to thirty troops and has a maximum takeoff weight of 28,660 lbs.

Source: *Jane's All The World's Aircraft, 1972-1973.*

numbers, their losses were much higher because the opposition enjoyed air superiority.

Little has been written concerning the role of Israeli helicopter forces, described last year as a keenly trained and highly spirited group armed with some of the most modern weapons available.[52] Presumably they performed relatively well, but the details of their activities apparently are not yet being disclosed.

In terms of manpower, Israel remains at a quantitative disadvantage (see Table 7), and its previous qualitative advantage has certainly decreased: Syrian and Egyptian troops proved quite capable of exploiting combat situations in the October conflict. Indeed, it has been said that a vast improvement has occurred in the leadership, morale, and general quality of Egyptian and Syrian troops since the 1967 war.[53] One example of improved training is that Arab troops

[52] Jac Weller, "Israeli Paratroopers," *Military Review*, March 1973, pp. 49-50.
[53] "Egypt Anchors Links," *Christian Science Monitor*, 19 October 1973, and Drew Middleton, "Who Lost the Yom Kippur War?" *Atlantic*, March 1974, p. 50.

Table 7

ARMY STRENGTHS IN THE MIDDLE EAST PRIOR
TO THE OCTOBER WAR

Country	Numbers
Egypt	260,000
Syria	120,000
Jordan	68,000
Iraq	90,000
Algeria	55,000
Libya	20,000
Saudi Arabia	36,000
Israel	275,000 [a]

[a] At full mobilization, which takes 72 hours.

Source: *Military Balance 1973-1974.*

were particularly effective in the use of shoulder-fired SAMs and antitank weapons. Indeed, American defense officials have indicated that the troops handling the SA-7s had to have advanced technical expertise in order to avoid Israeli decoy attempts.[54]

Even though the gap has begun to close, Arab forces still suffer from an inability to move considerable numbers of troops forward in any rapid offensive because of inadequate air cover. Thus the nearly two-to-one edge in helicopters and the much greater troop strength of the Arabs are of small importance as long as Tel Aviv continues to exercise aerial dominance.

Armor. Israeli control of the skies also greatly decreases the importance of the Arab numerical advantage in armor (see Tables 8 and 9). The lack of air protection leaves any forward Arab thrusts naked to Israeli airborne attacks with TOW antitank weapons, Maverick air-to-surface weapons, Hobo, Rockeye, and Walleye 1 stand-off weapons, and 30-mm. cannon. Furthermore, the TOW and Maverick are said to have better guidance systems and range than the Soviet-supplied Snapper and Sagger wire-guided antitank missiles that were apparently so successful in the first week of the war,[55] knocking out

---

[54] "SA-7 Avoids Flares," p. 17.

[55] Robert Hotz, "The Mideast Surprise," *Aviation Week and Space Technology,* 15 October 1973, p. 7, and "Soviet Aid Sparks Arab Gains," *Aviation Week and Space Technology,* 15 October 1973, p. 12.

Table 8

NUMBER OF TANKS IN THE MIDDLE EAST PRIOR
TO THE OCTOBER WAR

Country/Vehicle Type	1968	1973
Egypt		
JS-3	20	30
T-62	—	100
T-54/55	250	1,650
T-34	70	100
Pt-76	—	75
Centurion Mark 3	30	—
Total	370	1,955 [a]
Syria		
JS-3	—	30
T-54/55	—	900
T-34	200	240
T-54	150	—
Pt-76	—	100
Old German tanks	50	—
Total	400	1,270 [b]
Jordan		
M-60	—	} 200
M-47 and M-48	—	
Centurion	50	220
M-48	50	—
Total	100	420
Israel		
M-60	—	150
M-48	225	400
Ben Gurion	250	250
Centurion	—	600
Isherman and Super Sherman	—	200
Super Sherman	175	—
AMX-13	140	—
TI-67	—	100
T-54	200	—
Total	990	1,700 [c]

[a] According to losses reported during the war, Cairo had a much larger number of T-62s.

[b] Reported war losses indicate that Syria also possessed a number of T-62s.

[c] Based on war reports, Israel probably possessed a larger number of M-60s.

Source: *Military Balance 1967-1968* and *1973-1974.*

Table 9
CHARACTERISTICS OF MAJOR TANKS IN THE MIDDLE EAST

Type	Characteristics
T-62	This is believed to be standard equipment in the Soviet armored forces. It has a 115-mm. smooth-bore gun and a top speed of about 30 mph. It can cross water up to about eighteen feet in depth and has night-vision equipment.
T-54/55	Some are still in service with the Soviet armored forces. It is equipped with a 100-mm. gun and has a road speed of about 30 mph. It can cross water up to about eighteen feet in depth and has night-vision equipment.
Pt-76	The Pt-76 is a light amphibious tank used as the main reconnaissance vehicle of the Soviet army. It is capable of operating in a fast-flowing river or the open sea. It is considered mobile but it has limitations as a fighting vehicle. Armor protection is less than that of other light tanks. This vehicle has a 76-mm. low-velocity gun and a road speed of about 25 mph. It apparently has no night-vision equipment.
M-60	The M-60 is currently a main battle tank of the United States Army. It has a 105-mm. high-velocity gun and a top speed of about 30 mph. It can cross water up to about thirteen feet in depth and has night-vision equipment. The M-60's cross-country mobility is said to be inferior to more modern European tanks.
M-48	The M-48 is the main tank armament of the U.S. Marine Corps. It has a 90-mm. M-41 gun and a road speed of about 30 mph. Night-vision equipment can be fitted.
Centurion (Mark 13)	After twenty years of use, this tank is being phased out of the British army. The most recent version has a 105-mm. gun and can move at speeds up to about 20 mph. It is fitted with night-vision equipment, and can be fitted with water-crossing equipment.
Ben Gurion	This tank is similar to the Centurion, but the Israelis have replaced the original gun with a French 105-mm. gun.
Super Sherman	This is the old American Sherman tank modernized by Israel with the addition of French medium-velocity tank guns and new diesel engines. The majority of guns fitted are 105-mm., some are 75-mm. Road speed is less than 30 mph. Comparatively thin armor makes the Super Sherman vulnerable to the 100-mm. guns of the T-54/55.
Isherman	This is a rebuilt Sherman tank with a French 105-mm. gun and new engines for increased speed.[a] It is probably very similar to the Super Sherman.
TI-67	Equipped with a 105-mm. gun, this is the Israeli conversion of captured T-54/55 tanks.
Tsabar (or Sabra)	Unconfirmed reports indicate that Israel has this main battle tank in development. It is said to be fitted with a British 105-mm. gun and designed specifically for desert conditions. It may have already entered service with Israeli armored forces.

[a] Christopher Foss, *Armoured Fighting Vehicles of the World* (New York: Scribner, 1971), p. 68.

Source: Unless otherwise noted, information was derived from *Jane's Weapon Systems, 1972-1973.*

some 500 Israeli tanks. The RPG-7, a bazooka-type antitank weapon, also took its toll of Israeli armor.[56] During the war, Israeli forces also received American antitank rockets for infantrymen.[57]

The performance of tanks vis-à-vis the new missiles raises serious questions relative to the large-scale utilization of armor. Indeed, unless a tank can be built that is immune to such missile attacks, one may well see a decrease in the mass employment of this type of weapon.[58] Still, if armor is used to a great extent in future conflicts, Israel will probably maintain an advantage.[59]

Although Tel Aviv was caught technologically napping, unprepared to face or use antitank weapons on a large scale, it was able to avoid a military nightmare.[60] In turn, the United States responded in typical fashion, not only shipping Israel a greater number of tanks than it lost, but also providing it with antiarmor weapons which are considered to be superior to those possessed by the Arabs.[61]

Thus Israel appears to have an advantage in terms of antitank weapons, and its superiority in the skies gives it a tremendous

---

[56] Robert R. Ropelewski, "Egypt Assesses Lessons of October War," *Aviation Week and Space Technology*, 17 December 1973, p. 16.

[57] "U.S. Reports Antitank Missile Has Worked Well," *London Times*, 23 October 1973.

[58] According to American Defense Secretary Schlesinger, the United States is already developing a new tank (the XM-1) which promises increased survivability against modern antitank weapons. Schlesinger, *Defense Report*, FY 1975, p. 105.

[59] Israel is apparently still intending to utilize a large number of tanks and shortly after the October conflict was reportedly planning to double the number of tanks it possessed prior to the war. See Corddry, "Israel to Double Tank and Air Forces."

[60] The Israeli lack of preparedness was underscored by the Agranat Commission which was created to investigate Israeli military mishaps relative to the October war. The commission's findings included the recommendation that Chief of Staff General David Elazar be dismissed reportedly because he was held "responsible for erroneous evaluation of intelligence reports on the eve of the war and lack of preparedness of the Israeli Army." See Yuval Elizur, "Israel War Probe Hits Elazar," *Washington Post*, 3 April 1974.

[61] Estimates vary as to how many additional tanks the Israelis have received. Joseph Fried says that, according to Defense Minister Moshe Dayan, Tel Aviv now has 15 percent more tanks than before the war (Fried, "Israel Holds Edge"). Assuming that most of the American tank production increases are attributable to the resupply of Israel, some 500 M-60s alone may have been supplied to Tel Aviv as well as more than 155 earlier-model M-60s or M-48s. In terms of the latter it has been said that the U.S. Army may well purchase an additional 155 M-60s "with the funds received from the sale of less costly, earlier model tanks to Israel." Estimates were derived from the Schlesinger *Defense Report*, FY 1975, p. 104. No mention was made relative to how many M-48 tanks were shipped to Israel or the number of Soviet-built tanks captured by Tel Aviv.

advantage: its air force should be able to inflict heavy losses against any advancing Arab armor. In addition, it has been said that Israeli tanks seriously outgun those of the Arabs.[62] Furthermore, few would deny that Israeli troops are more skilled in the utilization of armor. The loss of over one-quarter of the tank force, however, must have also included a high percentage of casualties in the ranks of Israel's most experienced tankers.

The effectiveness of armored personnel carriers (APCs) has, of course, been decreased by the availability of antitank missiles. Nevertheless, the two superpowers apparently have replaced all losses of both tanks and APCs, and the three contiguous Arab states may hold a small quantitative advantage (see Tables 10 and 11), although Israeli Defense Minister Moshe Dayan reportedly has indicated that Tel Aviv now has 85 percent more APCs than before the October war.[63]

One of the most striking results of the October war is that the style of ground warfare has definitely changed: any future conflict will undoubtedly witness the use of greater numbers of missiles, not only against planes and helicopters, but also against armor. Consequently, both sides seem to be preparing for possible future hostilities by procuring large amounts of such weapons, and, in classical Middle East arms-race style, one side—Israel—has already taken the lead by getting more modern versions of those arms from the U.S. This, combined with Tel Aviv's air superiority and personnel

---

Table 10
NUMBER OF ARMORED PERSONNEL CARRIERS IN THE MIDDLE EAST PRIOR TO THE OCTOBER WAR

Country	Vehicle Type	Number
Egypt	BTR-40, 50P, 60, 152 and OT-64	2,000
Syria	BTR 50/60 and 152	1,000
Jordan	M-113	280
	Saracen	120
Israel	M-113 and salvaged captured APCs	Over 3,000 [a]

a Kenneth S. Bower, "The Israeli Armored Corps," *Armor*, May-June 1973, p. 21.
Source: Unless otherwise noted, *Military Balance 1973-1974*.

---

[62] Kenneth Hunt, "The Military Lessons," *Survival*, January/February 1974, p. 7, and Kenneth Bower, "The Israeli Armor Corps," *Armor*, May-June 1973, p. 21. It should also be noted that Israel is reportedly developing a main battle tank called Tsabar. *Jane's Weapon Systems*, 1972-1973, p. 255.
[63] Fried, "Israel Holds Edge."

Table 11

MAJOR CHARACTERISTICS OF ARMORED
PERSONNEL CARRIERS

Type	Characteristics
BTR-60	This Soviet-built amphibious armored personnel carrier can transport ten-to-thirteen infantrymen, depending upon version. It has good cross-country performance in terrain favoring wheels, but the suspension is probably inadequate for hard driving over rough ground. The need for the crew to mount and dismount via top hatches is a tactical disadvantage. Road speed is about 50 mph. The BTR has a 14.5-mm. heavy machine gun and a 7.62-mm. machine gun in turret mountings. It can be fitted with a rocket/flare launcher and antitank rocket launchers. It has some night-vision devices.
BTR-50	The BTR-50 (Soviet-built) is similar in performance to the Pt-76 light amphibious tank. It can carry fifteen men (crew of three plus twelve infantrymen) all of whom must mount and dismount through roof openings. Road speed is about 25 mph. It can carry four machine guns of 14.5-, 12.7- or 7.62-mm. caliber. It is fitted with night-fighting equipment.
OT-64	This is a Czechoslovakian amphibious vehicle. It carries two crewmen plus twenty infantrymen and has a road speed of about 60 mph. Depending on version, 7.62-, 12.7-, or 14.5-mm. machine guns can be carried.
BTR-40	This Soviet-built vehicle carries a crew of five, including the driver, and has an amphibious capability. Its road speed is about 50 mph. It has one 7.62-mm. machine gun on a front mounting and sometimes another on a rear mounting. A variant can be used as a guided weapon vehicle for Snapper antitank missiles.
BTR-152	This is an early type of Soviet armored personnel carrier. It has a crew of two plus fifteen men and can be armed with 7.62-mm. or 12.7-mm. machine guns, or twin 14.5-mm. antiaircraft guns. Road speed is about 45 mph.
M-113	This is the current United States Army armored personnel carrier. It has amphibious capability, carries about thirteen men, including the driver, and has .50-caliber machine guns. Egress is via a rear door. Road speed is about 40 mph. Variants include mountings for antitank missiles, mortars, and flame throwers.
Saracen	This vehicle is standard with the British army. It carries ten infantrymen and has a road speed of about 45 mph. It is armed with a .30-caliber machine gun. It is said to have remarkable cross-country ability, especially on dry, hard terrain.

Source: *Jane's Weapon Systems, 1972-1973.*

skill, gives the Israelis a significant military advantage which will hold into the near future.

Artillery. Both sides hold large quantities of the most modern field guns available, and the superpowers seem to have replaced losses incurred in the October fighting. In fact, Israel is said to now have

25 percent more artillery pieces than before the October war.[64] In addition, Tel Aviv reportedly has developed an improved version of the American-produced 175-mm., self-propelled gun, giving the weapon a range of some thirty-four miles with a 105-pound, 155-mm. shell.[65] The modified self-propelled gun nullifies any advantage the Arabs might have derived from having the longest-range Soviet artillery, which has a reach of less than twenty miles. A sufficient number of these new weapons in operation could mean that future artillery barrages by Israel may have to be answered with Soviet-supplied, surface-to-surface missiles like the Frog. The Arab response would be escalatory in terms of sophistication, but, given Israeli air superiority, they would have no other alternative.

Thus, in the area of artillery too, the Arab quantitative advantage is offset by Israeli technology. Moreover, despite the significant improvement in Arab military performance during the October war, the Israelis still can operate artillery with greater skill and accuracy.

3. Middle East Naval Forces

At sea, the fruits of Israeli technology and manpower skill paid off handsomely during the October war. Despite being outnumbered nearly two-to-one by Syrian and Egyptian naval craft (see Table 12), the Israelis were highly successful defending against the Soviet-built Styx surface-to-surface missiles carried by Osa- and Komar-class patrol boats. Tel Aviv reportedly was able to counteract the Styx by virtue of a device the Israelis developed which jammed the missile on its ballistic curve.[66] Offensively the Israelis are said to have used their domestically produced surface-to-surface missile, the Gabriel, as a sea skimmer, with clutter from the waves confusing the Russian jamming system.[67] Tel Aviv claims the Gabriels, fired from its Reshef- and Saar-class boats, accounted for the sinking of thirteen Osa- and Komar-class boats.[68] Israeli naval losses were placed at three Saars destroyed by Styx missiles from Egyptian Komar boats.[69]

---

[64] Ibid.

[65] Col. R. D. Heinl, Jr., USMC (ret.), "Egyptian Confronted by Israeli Superguns," *Detroit News*, 22 June 1973.

[66] Herbert Coleman, "Gabriel Outmatches Soviet Styx in Mideast Engagement at Sea," *Aviation Week and Space Technology*, p. 20.

[67] Ibid.

[68] Ibid. The maneuvering and technical ability must have been considerable for the Israelis to achieve such successes because *Jane's Fighting Ships, 1972-1973* (New York: McGraw-Hill Book Company, 1972), lists the Styx range at 18 miles and the Gabriel at 12.

[69] Coleman, "Gabriel Outmatches Styx."

Table 12

NAVAL VESSELS IN THE MIDDLE EAST PRIOR TO THE OCTOBER WAR

Country/Vessel Type	1967-68	1973
Egypt		
Submarines	8	12
Submarine chasers	—	12
Destroyers	8	5
Escorts	12 [a]	4
Minesweepers	10	12
Landing craft	6	14
Osa-class missile patrol boats	7	12
Komar-class missile patrol boats	5	7
Motor torpedo boats	40	36
Total	96	114
Syria		
Minesweepers	2	3
Submarine chasers	—	2
Coastal patrol boats	3	2
Fast patrol boats [b]	15	—
Komar- and Osa-class missile patrol boats	—	6
Motor torpedo boats	—	12
Total	20	25
Israel		
Submarines	4	3 [c]
Destroyers	2	1
Antiaircraft frigate	1	—
Coastal escort	1	—
Landing craft	2	9
Fast missile patrol boats	—	12 + [d]
Motor torpedo boats	11	9
Small patrol boats	4	23
Seaward defense boats	5	—
Total	30	57 +

[a] This includes six coastal craft.

[b] This may include some Komar-class boats.

[c] Israel reportedly has three aged British submarines with three new missile-armed ones being built in Great Britain (*Aviation Week and Space Technology*, 4 June 1973, p. 57).

[d] Israel is producing its own missile-armed gunboat called Reshef. Completion of the first—not included in the twelve—was announced 4 February 1973 (*Washington Post*, 5 February 1973). The exact number produced is not known.

Source: *Military Balance 1967-1968* and *1973-1974*.

In terms of resupply, it is possible that the United States may have already sent missile patrol craft to Israel as replacements for the lost Saars. This would not be particularly surprising in light of congressional testimony by Admiral Thomas Moorer and Deputy Defense Secretary Elwood Clements that Washington had replaced Israeli naval losses. (The Reshef type presumably would not be included in that replacement category since it is produced in Israel.)

Elsewhere in the naval realm, Israel and Egypt appear to be developing submarine forces. In this area of naval power the Egyptians hold a substantial quantitative equipment edge, but Israel apparently will be making significant additions to its fleet. Three German-designed submarines are being built for Tel Aviv in Great Britain, and they will have a new British missile system that can be used against small attack vessels and antisubmarine warfare helicopters.[70] A major advantage of this submarine is that it is relatively small, which should enable it to operate effectively in the shallow south Mediterranean waters.[71]

Although quantitatively at a disadvantage, the Israelis are obviously more skilled in developing naval warfare techniques and applying them in a conflict situation. But in the October war, the two Arab naval forces showed considerable qualitative improvement and the Israeli technological innovation with the Gabriel system and related jamming capability apparently was the deciding factor. Still, Israel continues to hold an overall naval advantage which increases considerably when Tel Aviv's air superiority is taken into account: effectively armed and piloted aircraft can inflict heavy naval casualties.

4. Nuclear and CBR Scenarios

Considering the foregoing, it is obvious that there has been a significant arms race in the Middle East, particularly since the 1967 war, and that in the wake of the October conflict both sides have moved much faster toward rearmament and preparation for the outbreak of hostilities than toward peace. Indeed, by comparison, the rate of movement for peace could best be described as a snail's pace. So the large and impressive inventories of modern weapons carried by the Arabs and Israelis become especially significant with the high probability that these arms will be used in another war, one that promises

---

[70] "Israel Buys British Missile System," *Aviation Week and Space Technology,* 4 June 1973, p. 57.
[71] Ibid.

to result in an even greater level of destruction than the October conflict.

The probability of such a conflict becoming nuclear is also greater than before, and there is even a possibility that chemical, biological, or radiological (CBR) warfare tactics may be introduced in the next conflict. Given these contingencies, it is appropriate to consider some possible war scenarios that might occur with these types of nuclear and unconventional warfare, and to examine the various weapons now in the inventories of probable future belligerents.

To some it may appear ironic that the American-supplied weapons in the Israeli inventories, which were intended to give Tel Aviv a military advantage, may ultimately lead to the use of nuclear weapons in the Middle East. For instance, if the Arabs, out of frustration over a lack of progress in the peace talks aimed at regaining the territory seized by Israel in 1967, decide to reopen hostilities, it will likely include the use of their Soviet-supplied Scud missiles, and, as mentioned previously, even a relatively few of these surface-to-surface missiles with high-explosive warheads could rain considerable destruction upon Israel.[72] The use of these weapons by the Arabs would undoubtedly be predicated on the knowledge that their equipment and pilots are no match for Israel's and that the missiles therefore present the most effective military option remaining. Should the Scuds be relatively effective, or if Israeli forces are generally suffering a turning in the tide of battle against themselves, it is possible that Tel Aviv would unleash the 280-mile range Jericho surface-to-surface missile with nuclear warheads,[73] or deliver such bombs with F-4 Phantom aircraft.[74] Any Israeli use of atomic weapons, however, would be almost certain to cause a Soviet intervention on behalf of its client states, which would probably in turn lead to a reaction by the United States.

Of course, the use of nuclear weapons in the Middle East is not exclusively an Israeli option, but before the Arabs could launch a nuclear strike they would have to procure the warheads, and thus far

---

[72] See De Borchgrave, "Sadat's Vision."

[73] For a more extensive treatment of the Israeli nuclear and missile capability see Tahtinen, *Arab-Israeli Balance*, pp. 32-36; Schmidt, "Nuclear Stockpile"; and Smith Hempstone, "Why Israel Pulled Back," Washington *Star-News*, 29 March 1974. The latter reports that Israel has "perfected a simple, inexpensive means of producing the enriched uranium necessary for nuclear weapons."

[74] In 1968 when Israel was negotiating for some fifty F-4s, it reportedly asked that some of the planes be equipped with nuclear bomb racks. Hendrick Smith, "U.S. Assumes Israelis Have A-Bomb or Its Parts," *New York Times*, 18 July 1970.

the Soviet Union has given no appearance of being willing to provide such weapons to its client states. One thing is certain, however: the Arabs are extremely nervous about the possibility of Israel using nuclear weapons. But, once again, superiority by one side does not lessen the chances of conflict. Indeed, at least one leading Arab has called for his government to procure such warheads to serve as a counter-threat.[75]

Another possibility is that when Israeli or Arab forces have suffered serious battlefield setbacks they may turn to the use of gas or more serious CBR warfare.[76] In fact, either side may utilize such weapons before exercising the nuclear option, or they may decide to use them in conjunction. In the October war, Soviet-supplied military equipment gave the Arabs an extensive capability for defense against CBR attacks, which led United States Army Chief of Staff General Creighton Abrams to refer to it as "one of the most impressive lessons of the conflict." [77] He was quoted as telling the House Armed Services Committee that the army was surprised by the "sophistication, completeness and extensiveness of these defenses." [78]

Thus, the Middle East arms race appears to have taken an even more serious, and potentially disastrous, turn. This leads to several very thought-provoking questions: Have the Israelis developed a CBR capability and have the Soviets and Arabs become convinced that Tel Aviv might use it? Or, are the Soviets planning to supply their Arab clients with such weapons? [79]

There is little doubt that the Israelis possess the technical manpower base to develop such weapons, and it is possible—though highly unlikely—that the United States provided Tel Aviv with offensive or defensive CBR equipment. There is also the possibility that, as in the ECM field,[80] Israel may have brought in a number of experts to assist in building such a capability.

---

[75] For example, shortly before his removal as the editor of Egypt's semi-official newspaper, *Al Ahram*, Mohammed Hussenein Haykal issued such a call.

[76] When Israeli troops were recently ordered to cut off their hair and beards, the justification was that in the event of gas warfare the excess hair would prevent the soldiers from putting on their gasmasks. Andrew Borowiec, "Israel's Army Ponders Strategy in New Context," Washington *Star-News*, 14 January 1974.

[77] John W. Finney, "Abrams Cites Intelligence from Soviet Arms in Mideast," *New York Times*, 15 February 1974.

[78] Ibid.

[79] During the Yemeni war in 1962 Egyptian troops allegedly used some type of poison gas. See "Cairo Said to Use Gas Bombs," *New York Times*, 9 July 1963, and "6 Gas Deaths Listed by Yemen Royalists," *New York Times*, 12 July 1963.

[80] "Eased Export Policy Realization Lags," *Aviation Week and Space Technology*, 21 February 1972, p. 69.

Along with these nuclear and CBR warfare scenarios it is appropriate to consider some of the kinds of military equipment now in the Middle East that can be armed with these lethal weapons. The most obvious nuclear delivery systems are surface-to-surface missiles such as the Jericho and Scud, as well as smaller, shorter-range Frog-3s and -7s.[81] In terms of aircraft, the Israeli F-4s are the most capable of effectively delivering nuclear bombs.[82] On the ground, both sides possess various types of artillery which can fire nuclear or chemical shells. Among them are the American-supplied 155- and 105-mm. howitzers, the Soviet-produced 122- and 240-mm. howitzers, and Russian 240- and 160-mm. mortars.[83]

Thus, the Israeli capability of producing such lethal weapons and the possibility that Tel Aviv may be able to acquire additional delivery systems from the United States, combined with the chance —albeit slim at this time—that the Arabs may be able to eventually acquire nuclear and CBR weapons, adds another potential spark to the Middle East tinderbox.

5. American Involvement

In light of the numerous possible war situations, all of which could involve the United States in a confrontation with the Soviet Union, it is essential to consider how strong a commitment Washington has made to Tel Aviv.[84] In search of an answer one begins with the fact that there are no known treaties between the United States and Israel requiring direct American defense of the latter. Nevertheless, Washington's military involvement with Tel Aviv seems to be following the all too familiar pattern of constant escalation in an arms race which is blamed on the Soviets, even though they have yet to provide the same degree of offensive weaponry to any Arab country. Indeed, particularly since the 1967 war, Moscow seems to be caught in the position of having to react to more and more advanced offensive weapons provided to Tel Aviv by Washington.

It is especially noteworthy, however, that supplying new arms on a seemingly regular basis is not even the ultimate end to this

---

[81] *Jane's Weapon Systems, 1972-1973*, and *Jane's All the World's Aircraft, 1972-1973* (New York: McGraw-Hill Book Company, 1972).

[82] Ibid.

[83] *Jane's Weapon Systems, 1972-1973*, *Jane's Aircraft, 1972-1973*, and *Military Balance, 1973-1974*.

[84] The United States appears to have fewer options vis-à-vis its client state, since Israel has no other major source to which it can turn for sophisticated weapons.

apparently powerful informal commitment to Israel. Twice in the last seven years the United States has risked a nuclear confrontation with the U.S.S.R. because of strong American support for Israel. In 1967 Washington was willing to risk a nuclear conflagration even though Tel Aviv started the war with a large-scale attack against Egyptian airfields on 5 June. On the morning of 10 June, President Lyndon Johnson received a "hotline" message from Soviet Premier Alexei Kosygin, which indicated that if Tel Aviv did not halt its operations within a few hours the U.S.S.R. would undertake appropriate actions, including those of a military nature.[85] In response, orders which originally prohibited units of the American Sixth Fleet from approaching closer than 100 miles to the Syrian coast were changed by President Johnson, reducing the stand-off distance to about fifty miles,[86] and the fleet, with Soviet reconnaissance ships in shadowy pursuit, moved in. Thus, history records that the United States, at the risk of war, moved to provide protection to its client state.

The second time (October 1973) Washington was willing to chance a nuclear conflagration—and was presumably prepared to conduct such warfare—is probably still vivid in the minds of most readers. Although the American preparedness to come to the active military assistance of Israel was not implemented, it demonstrates once again the strength of U.S. commitments to Tel Aviv.

The October war was much more revealing of the American commitment than the 1967 conflict, probably because the Arab forces fought much better, challenging Israeli superiority, at least in the early days of hostilities. In the October fighting, the United States was so committed to helping Israel that it practically ignored the NATO allies, most of whom were unwilling to assist Tel Aviv or allow their countries to be used for staging bases for the resupply effort. The United States reportedly did not even consult with its NATO allies before placing American forces on alert.[87] The American commitment to Israel is apparently so strong that during the trans-Atlantic resupply effort, the United States, even though its own forces were ready to challenge the Soviets if necessary, seriously depleted the equipment stocks of some American units which, as a result, would, in the event of hostilities with the U.S.S.R., not have

[85] Lyndon Baines Johnson, *The Vantage Point* (New York: Holt, Rinehart and Winston, 1971), p. 302.

[86] Ibid.

[87] "NATO Tries To Bury the Hatchet on Lack of U.S. Consultation," *Aviation Week and Space Technology*, 17 December 1973, p. 22.

been as combat-ready as their Soviet counterparts.[88] Comparatively, although the Soviet resupply effort was quantitatively larger—which is not surprising in view of far greater Arab equipment losses—there is no reliable information indicating that Moscow's sacrifice from inventories and frontline forces was as significant as that made by Washington.

The intensity of Washington's commitment to Tel Aviv is also reflected in the degree to which the United States is willing to absorb extensive economic costs to keep Israel militarily superior. Indeed, the cost of the resupply—nearly all of which will be borne by the United States—may run as high as $5 billion by the time American military inventories are replaced. Furthermore, if the skyrocketing price of petroleum products and the cost of oil-shortage related unemployment is added to that figure, the true cost of the war to the United States is many times more than the armament expenditures. Finally, the supply of sophisticated weapons inevitably brings with it, regardless of the client state's military proficiency, a commitment of additional U.S. defense-related personnel either on a temporary or semi-permanent basis.

Washington's apparent commitment to keep Tel Aviv significantly stronger than the Arab states may have even resulted in Israel having greater numbers of more sophisticated weapons than before the October war. In fact, Tel Aviv's weapons edge vis-à-vis the Arabs may have actually increased. For instance, as previously mentioned, many of Israel's aircraft losses were replaced by flying in F-4s and A-4s, possibly in greater numbers than those lost. More significantly, however, if the planes were flown in they would not likely be included as part of the total resupply tonnage figure chalked up by American transport planes. Also not included in that figure are the many tons of military equipment transported by El Al aircraft and numerous ships of non-American registry. If one compares the amount of tonnage apparently transported to the Arab states with the tremendous losses suffered by Arab forces (nearly fourfold in terms of aircraft, well over twofold in armor [89]), then one finds that the magnitude of resupply operations leaned heavily in Israel's favor. This disparity widens considerably when it is realized that some of

---

[88] U.S. Army Chief of Staff General Creighton W. Abrams has reportedly said the army's "overall-readiness posture" was "adversely affected" when equipment and munitions from army inventories were sent to Israel last fall ("Abrams Cites Intelligence").

[89] Coleman, "Air Force Decisive in War," and "Cost of the War in Men and Machines," *London Times*, 26 October 1973.

the huge Arab aircraft losses were replaced with planes shipped in large Russian transport aircraft.[90]

6. If a Superpower War Occurs

Fortunately, in the October conflict none of the transports of either superpower were damaged enough by the warring states to cause military repercussions. In any future conflict, however, it is not hard to imagine a situation in which some of the suppliers' transport aircraft or vessels are attacked by one of the belligerents. In which case the response of the affected power—whether the United States or the Soviet Union—would likely be military, thereby leading to the strong probability of a confrontation between the nuclear giants.

With the possibility that the U.S.S.R. and the United States may become embroiled in a Middle East conflict, a consideration of their military strengths in that part of the world is in order. Although it is likely that the losing power would introduce nuclear weapons and widen the conflict, the emphasis in this comparison will be on the exploitation of the conventional warfare advantages held by Moscow and Washington within a scenario that limits war to the Middle East.

If the United States were to be victorious in any Middle East hostilities with the Soviet Union, heavy reliance would have to be placed on the American Sixth Fleet and the NATO allies. The American naval force would have to contend with a modern Soviet fleet manned by well-trained and highly motivated men, operating relatively close to its logistics base.[91] In comparison, the aging and numerically inferior American fleet has two important advantages: sea-based aircraft and personnel that have combat experience.[92]

The Soviet fleet, however, can be more quickly reinforced, and land-based Soviet naval aircraft as well as those from Southern Warsaw Pact air forces could raise havoc with the American Medi-

---

[90] The American C-5 *alone* is said to have carried nearly two-thirds the tonnage of the "entire competing Soviet airlift." David Brown, "Israel Airlift Flights Underscore C-5 Rapid Deployment Capability," *Aviation Week and Space Technology*, 10 December 1973, p. 16.

[91] Admiral Isaac C. Kidd, Jr., "View from the Bridge of the Sixth Fleet Flagship," *U.S. Naval Institute Proceedings*, February 1972, pp. 19-20. During the October war the American Sixth Fleet already appeared to be without adequate Mediterranean bunkering facilities. Thus, in any future Middle East hostilities the United States may have to rely on extended trans-Atlantic petroleum convoys which would be highly vulnerable to Soviet interdiction.

[92] Ibid., p. 20.

terranean force. Furthermore, with the use of airfields in Algeria, Libya, Egypt, Syria, and Iraq, Russian aircraft would have a large variety of bases from which to stage.

To offset these Soviet advantages the United States would have to depend heavily upon its NATO allies, and in this regard there is a critical question that must be asked: Would the NATO countries be willing to commit their forces against the U.S.S.R. if there were no attack against them? Considering the reaction of most NATO countries during the October conflict, the answer is probably no. Indeed, during that conflict these states ultimately ordered the United States to refrain from using their countries as staging bases for the resupply effort. Most of the NATO allies even went one step further and demanded that Israel return the territory it seized from the Arabs in the 1967 war.

Considering NATO's general opposition toward militarily assisting Israel during hostilities, it is somewhat surprising that the American secretary of defense would even seemingly imply that equipment intended for NATO theatre defense purposes might be used in a future Arab-Israeli conflict. He points out

> that once we have established our baseline requirements, we should test their adequacy against a number of "off-design" cases to see whether what can lick the cat can also lick the kitten. Indeed, we have recently had just such a test thrust upon us—and a very empirical one at that—in the form of the Middle East war. As it turned out, our attack carriers (used as enroute airfields) and our strategic airlift, bought for quite other purposes, proved themselves very smartly and efficiently in an "off-design" contingency.[93]

This, in turn, leads to a very important question, the answer to which could have grave implications for the future of U.S.-NATO relations. Is the United States planning to use forces and equipment committed to the defense of Western Europe in any future Middle Eastern war even though the NATO countries may object?

If the October war is a reflection of NATO reaction to any future Middle East conflict, then the United States would probably have to go it alone, and the results may well be disastrous. The importance of NATO assistance to the United States in any Middle East conflict should not be underestimated. A former commander of the Sixth Fleet has stated that "in view of the magnitude and capability" of the Soviet forces in the Mediterranean "the combined

---

[93] Schlesinger, *Defense Report, FY 1975*, p. 85.

support of the NATO navies becomes increasingly important."[94] The significance of that support is particularly evident when it is realized that in any war with the U.S.S.R. American reliance is placed upon NATO naval forces to protect logistic lines across the Mediterranean and that the alliance's Southern Striking Force is depended upon for the destruction of Soviet African bases.[95] Even with complete NATO cooperation, however, there is no guarantee of a Soviet defeat in the Mediterranean. Against Moscow's advantages in any such conflict, Washington would find it very difficult and costly to emerge victorious from a Middle East war. So if the United States becomes involved in even a limited conflict with the U.S.S.R. in Moscow's "backyard," the probability is very high that such a war would ultimately become nuclear.

Conclusion

Despite the greater challenge to Israel in the October war, Tel Aviv continues to maintain military superiority vis-à-vis its Arab neighbors and is likely to continue to do so for some time, particularly as long as the United States is willing to provide it with more sophisticated weaponry. This, combined with an apparent Soviet reluctance to ship highly advanced offensive arms to the Arabs, has allowed the Israelis to develop a sizable edge in the military balance of power. The greatest danger, however, is that the U.S.S.R. may for a variety of reasons decide to match American military equipment in the area, even going so far as to send in Russian forces during any future wars. Of course, the United States might also come to the active military assistance of its client state. The one certainty is that a breakneck arms race is going on in the Middle East, fueled by ideologies, geopolitical rivalries and military intelligence curiosities of the superpowers.[96] This makes it all the more imperative to reach a final peace settlement in the area.

The danger and costs that United States involvement in the Arab-Israeli conflict has engendered make it essential that the American public be better informed of its government's commitments to Israel. Indeed, there are a number of questions in this crucial foreign

---

[94] Ibid., p. 29.

[95] Ibid., pp. 22-23.

[96] Regarding the military intelligence curiosities of the superpowers, there can be little doubt that both the U.S. and U.S.S.R. have some interest in observing the performance of each other's more sophisticated weaponry in the Middle East setting.

policy area that should be frankly answered by our government. For example, what is the extent of our *direct* military commitment to Israel? Does the "off-design" contingency referred to by Defense Secretary Schlesinger mean that we are already planning to come to the military assistance of Israel in any future war even if it means antagonizing our NATO allies and possibly fighting without their assistance? With the provision of massive amounts of offensive weaponry, are there any controls that Washington has over Tel Aviv's possible military endeavors, including those of a nuclear nature? Would the United States again risk a military confrontation with the U.S.S.R. to protect Israeli forces? If the answer to the latter query is affirmative, would that support exist even if Tel Aviv were to move preemptively, as in the June 1967 war? Have we guaranteed Israel the protection of our nuclear umbrella, and, if so, is it a blanket agreement that is enforceable regardless of the circumstances surrounding any military actions in which Tel Aviv is involved?

As for Soviet commitments to direct intervention on behalf of the Arabs, should full-scale warfare erupt again, little if anything is apparently known beyond the reports of Russian conventional force alerts during the October war. This issue should, of course, be of high-priority concern in any U.S. military calculation for the Middle East.

APPENDIX

United States Military Lessons from the October War

Secretary of Defense James Schlesinger recently pointed out a number of military lessons which the United States learned from the Middle East conflict. The following excerpts from his latest defense report highlight those lessons.

Soviet actions during the October 1973 Middle East War show that detente is not the only, and in certain circumstances not the primary, policy interest of the USSR. The immediate Soviet arms shipments to Egypt and Syria at the outset of hostilities, the deployment of nuclear-capable SCUD missile launchers, the peremptory Soviet note to the United States Government implying the possibility of direct Soviet military intervention with ground and air forces, and the forward deployment of sizeable Soviet naval forces— over 90 Soviet ships in the Mediterranean at the height of the hostilities and smaller naval forces in the Indian Ocean —provided another lesson in Soviet willingness to take risks with world peace.

We also learned useful military lessons from the October hostilities. For example, the value of United States military capabilities—our capacity to airlift and sealift needed munitions and equipment over long distances, and the deterring presence of the Sixth Fleet—was proved. Our quick logistical response capabilities and large naval presence had much to do with moderating the effects of the war.

We learned both from our last campaigns in Vietnam and the ensuing force reductions after Vietnam, as well as from the Middle East crisis, that the readiness and level of modernization of our forces were not wholly adequate. With the support of the Congress, we are taking steps to correct this. Also, while our Middle East airlift effort was splendidly executed, we found our dependence on airlift highlighted. We need to increase that capability. . . .

In addition, the Middle East war confirmed prior judgments about various aspects of modern warfare. The principal points are:

— the importance of advanced warning and its assessment, and the ready forces available to take advantage of it;
— the heavy attrition of equipment and supplies that can result from modern, intense conventional conflict;
— the need for balanced, mutually supporting forces, i.e., not just tanks and aircraft, but infantry, antitank weapons, artillery and ground air defenses as well;
— the new importance of modern antitank and air defense weapons;
— the importance of defense suppression weapons, equipment and tactics;
— the importance of a warm [ready] production base, and sufficient reserve stocks of ammunition, spare parts and equipment;
— the importance of trained manpower.[1]

Schlesinger also emphasized the importance of different types of weapons systems based on lessons gleaned from the October hostilities. He pointed out:

The recent Middle East conflict reaffirmed our earlier conclusion that modern anti-tank weapons fired from the air as well as the ground can provide an effective counter to the modern tank. . . .

. . . The recent Middle East war again has demonstrated our tanks must not only be able to defeat the opposing tanks, they must also be able to survive against the opposing tanks and anti-tank weapons. In this respect, the new XM-1 should have a distinct advantage over our M60 series tanks. . . .

. . . The intensity and effectiveness displayed by the ground air defenses in the Middle East conflict impressed upon us even more compellingly the need to take still further actions to enhance the defense-suppression capabilities of our tactical forces. . . . by providing our tactical air forces with improved self-protection radar warning (RW) equipment, tactical electronic warfare (EW) support forces, and a greater number and variety of improved defense-suppression weapons and devices. . . .

---

[1] Excerpted from James R. Schlesinger, *Defense Report, FY 1975*, pp. 13-15.

. . . Our assessment of the results of the Middle East conflict has led us to the conclusion that the production of TOW and DRAGON anti-tank missiles should be substantially accelerated. . . .

. . . The Maverick air-to-ground (missile's) performance in the . . . Middle East conflict was quite impressive. . . .

. . . The Israeli Air Force has demonstrated, chaff, if used properly and in sufficient quantities, is an effective means of aircraft self-protection even against high density SAM defenses.[2]

Soviet Military Lessons from the October War

In this section an attempt will be made to show what military lessons the Soviet Union may have learned from the latest large-scale hostilities in the Middle East. Perhaps not surprisingly, the Soviet press has refrained from discussing the war in that context, but it is still possible to gain considerable insight into what were probably interpreted by Moscow as valuable military lessons learned during the conflict.[3]

First, the Soviet Union obviously gained considerable practical knowledge relative to the performance of the vast array of its military equipment which was used by the Arab forces. In many ways, Soviet military lessons evolving from the October conflict are parallel to those gleaned by the United States. As pointed out in the text of this study, the Middle East battlefields were filled with modern sophisticated weapons supplied by the superpowers, and, therefore, not surprisingly, the war was probably very instructive relative to the strengths and weaknesses of the different types of equipment used.

On the ground, the Russian T-62 and T-54/55 tanks and the various armored personnel carriers received valuable combat trials in conjunction with a military plan that included the utilization of antitank weapons. In this realm, antitank weapons with names such as Snapper, Sagger, and RPG-7 proved to be highly effective in

---

[2] Ibid., pp. 101, 106-107, 142-143, 152 and 154.

[3] U.S.S.R. radio broadcasts have emphasized the importance of high-quality Soviet equipment and training provided to Arab troops. Also, during the October war, *Krasnaya Zvezda* highlighted the same theme in an article by Colonel A. Leontyev, "When a Mirage Evaporates . . . ." In February *Krasnaya Zvezda* again emphasized the value of Soviet assistance to the Arabs in an article by Colonel A. Khorev, "Echo of the Suez Battles."

destroying a significant number of Israeli tanks.[4] However, by the same token, when American-supplied antiarmor weapons entered the war in large numbers, Soviet-built armor was highly vulnerable and suffered heavy losses.[5] Consequently, Moscow was able to gain knowledge not only about its own armor and antitank weapons, but it also had the chance to see how well the best American tanks and many of Washington's most advanced antiarmor weapons performed. The U.S.S.R. also had an opportunity to learn how effectively some of its advanced water-crossing equipment functioned when Egyptian forces relatively successfully utilized such bridging equipment to cross the Suez Canal in their quest to recapture control of the waterway and the Sinai.[6]

In the air, Moscow witnessed the inferiority of its MiG-21 in battle against Israeli aircraft.[7] While the Soviets were undoubtedly aware of the limitations of the MiG-21, the war gave them additional opportunities to view what equipment improvements were placed on the American F-4s and A-4s.

In terms of air defense the Soviets probably gained valuable insights into how to use the SA-7 more effectively and how to make the Russian-interlaced ZSU-23, SA-2, -3, and -6 air-defense system even more efficient. At the very least, Soviet military experts had the opportunity of witnessing the use of sophisticated American ECM against the Russian-supplied system.[8] Therefore, theoretically, Moscow should be able to develop future air defenses even more difficult for American ECM to operate against.

At sea, the U.S.S.R. probably learned some valuable lessons in terms of how vulnerable their Styx missiles are to jamming, the limitations of their own ECM on the Osa- and Komar-class missile boats, and the general maneuverability of such craft in an actual combat situation. However, as was pointed out in the text of this study, the naval aspect of the war was not as significant as those of air and land.

---

[4] Ibid. Also, see Ropelewski, "Egypt Assesses Lessons of October War," p. 16, and Hotz, "Lessons of October," p. 13.

[5] Ibid. Also, see "U.S. Reports Antitank Missile Has Worked Well," *London Times*, 23 October 1973.

[6] A *Krasnaya Zvezda* editorial published on 7 December 1973 reprinted an interview with the Egyptian general staff chief regarding the canal-crossing operation. Also, see Coleman, "Air Force Decisive in War," p. 20.

[7] Ibid., pp. 18-19.

[8] Israeli use of ECM was alluded to in early November by Lieutenant General Mikhail Naumenko in a *Krasnaya Zvezda* article entitled "Dispelling a Myth." Also see the Air Defense section of the text of this study.

More generally, although the attempt to recapture the occupied territories was planned and initiated by Arab forces, few would question that there was a large infusion of Soviet operational advice and, certainly, manpower training. Consequently, it is not surprising that the tactics employed by the Arabs were similar to traditional Soviet military doctrine, particularly the caution with which large Arab armored forces moved once they succeeded in crossing the canal. On neither front was there any large-scale attempt to pursue daring tactics—such as moving away from the protective air-defense umbrella—even in the early days of the war when the Israelis were in retreat. Thus, the Soviets had an opportunity to witness the virtues and limitations of at least some of its military doctrine as applied by the Arab forces.

The U.S.S.R. also had an opportunity to utilize its quick-reaction transport and resupply capability. Arab losses, which were far greater than those of Israel, necessitated a more extensive resupply operation, and the Soviets were able to see how effectively their forces could carry out a large-scale resupply effort. In addition, Moscow undoubtedly recognized the need for keeping a ready production base and sufficient inventory of reserve equipment, spare parts, and ammunition.

Cover and book design: Pat Taylor